A World Cookbook

by Rachel Russ

illustrated by JiaJia Hamner

OXFORD
UNIVERSITY PRESS

Take a trip around the world. Find out fantastic facts and sample tasty foods.

This book shares simple versions of recipes from across the globe. Try some yourself!

Italy

This is the flag of Italy.

The capital city of Italy is Rome.

There are three active **volcanoes** in Italy, including Mount Etna.

Food Fact

Italy is well known for its food. This includes mouth-watering pasta, pizza and ice cream.

Pasta with Cheese and Pepper

You will need:

2 handfuls of pasta

1 handful of cheese

Pepper

Butter

When you see this, get an adult to help!

Method:

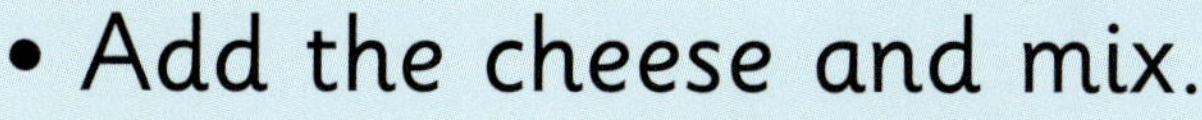

- Cook the pasta in boiling water.
- Melt the butter in a pan.
- Add a little pepper.
- Drain the pasta and add it to the butter.
- Add the cheese and mix.

Canada

Canada is huge! It is in the continent of North America. There are rocky peaks, lakes and icy mountains in Canada.

Canada is home to lots of interesting wildlife. There are bears, arctic foxes and cougars.

bear

arctic fox

cougar

Food Fact

Maple syrup is a **sap** collected from maple trees.

Pancakes with Maple Syrup

You will need:

1 cup of milk

1 and a half cups of plain flour

2 eggs

Butter

Maple syrup

Method:

- Mix the egg and milk in a jug.
- Gradually, stir the mix into the flour.
- Heat butter in a pan.
- Add some batter.
- When it bubbles, flip the pancake.
- Serve with maple syrup.

China

China is huge, too! One third of China is covered in mountains.

China is the only place where pandas live in the wild. The giant panda is China's national animal.

Food Fact

Traditionally, people in China use **chopsticks** to eat.

Vegetable Noodles

You will need:

2 handfuls of cooked noodles

1 carrot

1 teaspoon of soy sauce

1 teaspoon of honey

Oil

Half a cup of frozen peas

Method:

- Grate the carrot.
- Mix the soy and honey.
- Heat oil in a pan.
- Add the noodles and vegetables.
- Add the sauce and mix well.

Mexico

Mexico has high peaks and deep **canyons**. In the north, there are deserts. In the south, there are lush rainforests.

The Cardon cactus is the tallest cactus in the world. It grows in Mexico.

Food Fact

Mexico was the first place where sweetcorn was grown to eat.

Sweetcorn Salad

You will need:

2 large tomatoes

1 handful of salad leaves

Half a cup of sweetcorn

Half a cup of kidney beans

1 lime

Method:

- Chop the tomatoes into small chunks.
- Put the salad leaves into a large bowl.
- Add the tomatoes, sweetcorn and beans.
- Squeeze the lime over everything.
- Mix well and serve.

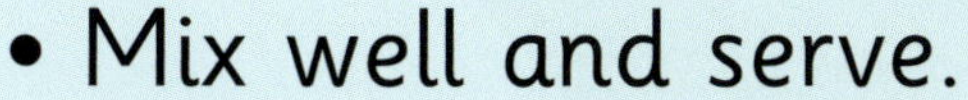

Jamaica

Jamaica is in the Caribbean Sea. Jamaica has white sandy beaches, forest-covered peaks and coral reefs.

The national bird of Jamaica is the red-billed streamertail.

Food Fact

A plantain looks like a banana. It is firmer and not as sweet.

Plantain

You will need:

1 plantain

Oil

Cinnamon
or nutmeg (optional)

Method:

- Chop the plantain into slices.
- Heat oil in a pan.
- Fry the plantain.
- Place the plantain on a paper towel. This will **absorb** any oil.
- Sprinkle the spice over the plantain.

Glossary

absorb: to soak up

canyons: deep rocky valleys, often with rivers at their bases

chopsticks: small, smooth sticks for eating, used like pincers in one hand

sap: thick, sticky liquid inside a tree or other plant

volcanoes: rocky peaks with openings where hot melted rock comes out

Index